D1482677

917.53   ✓ 79-11991
   M
Manley, Nick
   American photo album, Washington.

AMERICAN PHOTO ALBUM

WASHINGTON

AMERICAN PHOTO ALBUM
WASHINGTON
NICK MANLEY

EAST
50
Washington

PEEBLES PRESS
New York · London

First Published 1977 by
Peebles Press International, Inc.
10 Columbus Circle, New York,
New York 10019

DESIGNED BY NICOLAI CANETTI

© 1977 Peebles Press International, Inc.
ISBN 0-672-52362-0
Library of Congress Catalogue Card
Number 77-75354

Photographs appearing on pages 5,
76, 82 (top), 84 (top)
courtesy of the Washington Area Convention
and Visitors Association.

Distributed by
The Bobbs-Merrill Co., Inc.
4300 West 62nd St.,
Indianapolis, Indiana 46268, U.S.A.

Barrie & Jenkins
24 Highbury Crescent
London N5 1RX, England
in the U.K., Ireland, Australia,
New Zealand and South Africa

Printed and bound in the
United States of America

"This city is set up very nicely for the tourist. You come into Union Station and as soon as you get off your train there's the National Visitor Center, then you go outside and the tourmobile comes by right in front of the Center . . . you get on and it takes you all around the city to the sights. If you have your car you drive around the parkways which wind in through the monuments and Capitol Hill and across the river to Arlington Cemetery and Virginia. A visit to Washington makes a wonderful vacation for a family or anyone who wants to get back in touch with what the country's all about. You leave the city with an enormous sense of pride."

—Visitor on Third Trip to Washington

"At the Lincoln Memorial, well, it's very solemn when there's no people around . . . You can go up there and really understand what the country's all about."

—Groundskeeper

"Especially at night the monuments are incredibly beautiful . . ."

—Guard at Lincoln Memorial

"No matter how many times I see Lincoln sitting up there . . . I still get a shiver down my back . . . when I look up at him y'know . . ."

—Fireman

"I like the view of the Washington monument you get here better in the day than at night . . . it's very impressive, what's even more impressive is that it was built with contributions from the public all through the 1800's which just shows the gratitude of the people of the United States for the father of their country."

—Congressional Aide

"With the moon coming up in the reflection pool . . . it's awe-inspiring . . . simply awe-inspiring. We've come a long way to see this." —Californian

"It's just about the most romantic thing . . . driving along the Potomac at night . . . all those lights on the water . . . it just puts you in the greatest mood . . . oh, it's so dreamy." —Telephone Operator

"This is one city where the tallest building is not a skyscraper but a monument . . . the Washington Monument . . . you might say it's like Washington himself—it stands head and shoulders above everything else." —Embassy Administrator

"When you look up at Thomas Jefferson . . . it's inspiring to think that he's in the direct line of the White House, so anyone in the Oval Office can see the statue and be renewed." —Elementary School Teacher

"It's a nice leisurely walk from the Jefferson Memorial over to the Lincoln Memorial . . ." —Customs Official, Treasury Department

"It's a great honor to be here. There's only 18 of us . . . it's guarded twenty-four hours a day and we all feel it's a great honor to be chosen."

—Corporal of the Guard, Tomb of the Unknown Soldier

"After a busy day, when the tourists have left; say 5:00-5:30, and the sun is so that there's a lot of shade . . . the cemetery gets very quiet, very tranquil and very serene. It's really very beautiful, the best time of the day for me."

—Female Guard, Arlington Cemetery

"It's an exciting place to work, you're driving around such a historical area."

—Manager, Washington Park Service

"I like looking at the statues and riding around on things." —Nine Year Old Girl

"Some people claim that we have a ghost here. I think that's interesting . . . and a couple of people have said that they've even seen the ghost up in Section 13 where the oldest graves are. When you think about it, this city has a lot of legends."

—Caretaker, Arlington Cemetery

"*I think everyone has his favorite of the monuments . . . if you live here you can pick one out and say . . . that's my monument . . . that one says it all . . .*"

—Bank Teller

"*L'Enfant was one of the great pioneers of the city . . . his plans laid the groundwork for Washington . . . one of the reasons the city is as beautiful as it is . . .*" —City Co-ordinator, National Council for the Arts

"*The Iwo Jima Memorial was special. I'm a veteran of two wars and seeing that statue really hit home for me.*" —Retired Major, U.S. Army

PIERRE CHARLES L'ENFANT
ENGINEER ARTIST SOLDIER
UNDER THE DIRECTION OF
GEORGE WASHINGTON
DESIGNED THE PLAN FOR THE
FEDERAL CITY

MAJOR U.S. ENGINEER CORPS 1795
CHARTER MEMBER OF THE
SOCIETY OF THE CINCINNATI
DESIGNED ITS CERTIFICATE & INSIGNIA

BORN IN PARIS, FRANCE, AUGUST 2, 1755
DIED JUNE 14, 1825
WHILE RESIDING AT
CHILHAM CASTLE MANOR
PRINCE GEORGE'S CO. MARYLAND
AND WAS INTERRED THERE

RE-INTERRED AT ARLINGTON
APRIL 28, 1909

"Pierce Mill is a real achievement . . . a Washington landmark . . . it's amazing the way they bring history to life . . . as you walk around you feel as though you stepped back to another time." —Journalist

"Ever since I moved to Washington, my friends from other cities are always down here visiting. People consider the city exciting and there really is a lot of things to do. I never run out of places to take them." —Senate Intern

"I think there's a lot of things in Washington that you can see for free that you can't see in other cities." —Day Care Worker

"Culturally, I can't imagine any city more stimulating . . . there's Folger Shakespeare Center which does all the Shakespeare things, and outdoor theater in the parks, and Ford's Theatre where Lincoln was shot. If you like going to museums there's the Smithsonian . . . the National Gallery, Hirshhorn Museum . . . and Wahingtonians really go to all these places, they're not there just for the tourists, the people here in the city really enjoy going out, keeping up with the new events and exhibits." —Administrative Assistant, Pentagon

"Washington is a very liveable city . . . business, politics, recreation, cultural events and great people bring the city to life . . . what more could you ask?"
—Administrative Assistant, Department of Agriculture

"Maybe someone might think D.C. wouldn't be much of a town for a person in show business . . . well, I happen to know the people here like to go out and have a nice time, I mean I'm a singer and I always get a terrific response from the audience, it's a very warm city, well it's pretty sophisticated too, but still very warm people." —Nightclub Singer

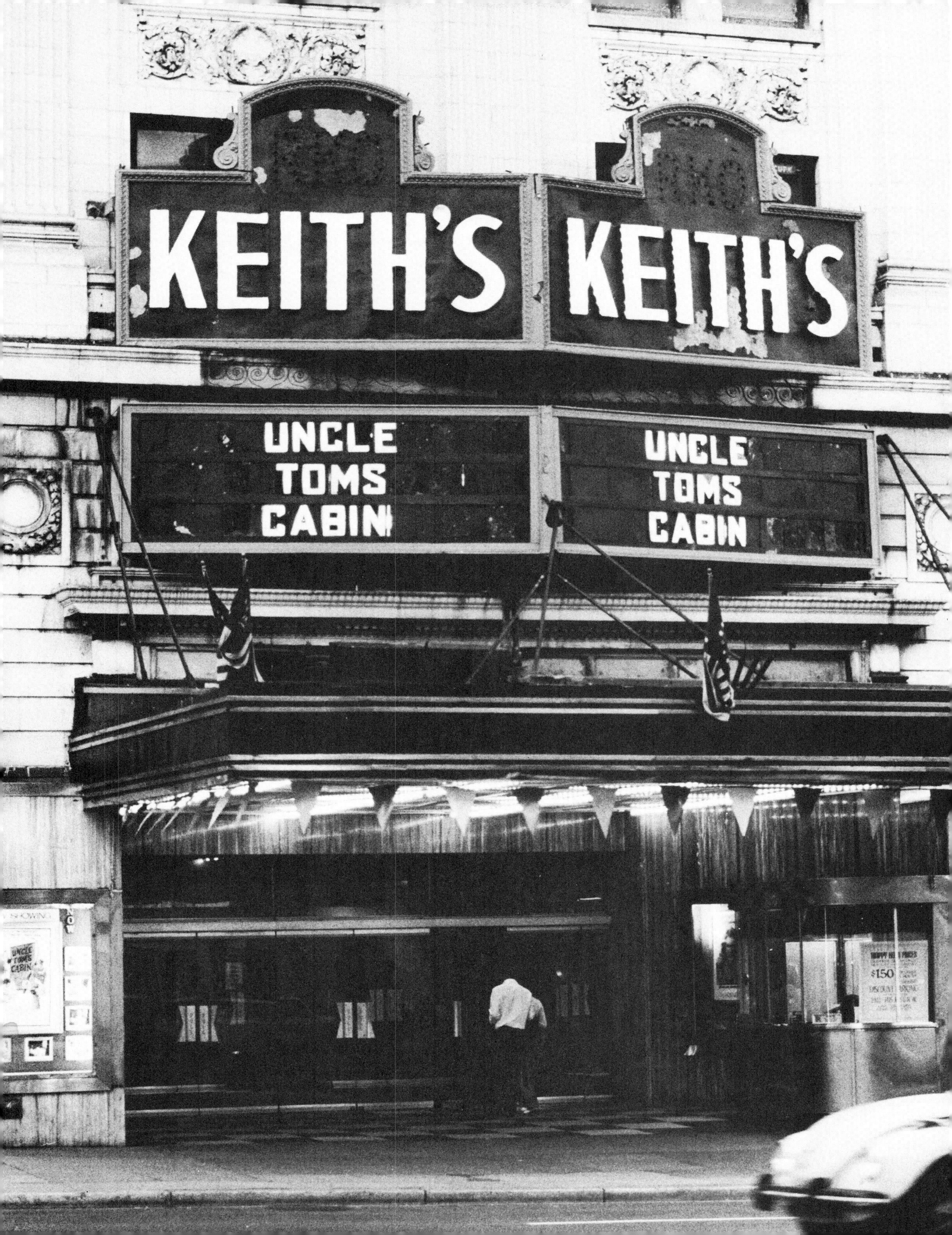
KEITH'S
KEITH'S
UNCLE TOMS CABIN
UNCLE TOMS CABIN

"*The city's sure pretty. I think the highlight of our trip will be the Smithsonian . . . that's what we mostly came for.*" —Texan

"*It's a great place to bring up a family. The kids never get tired of playing in the parks and taking trips to the museums.*" —Housewife

"*I consider a trip to Washington a delight. I've been coming here for many years. This is my sixteenth trip with the students.*" —Teacher, Ohio

41

"When we made this trip to Washington we knew we wanted to see Ford's Theatre and the house where he died; it was sad to think about it afterwards, but seeing the theater and Petersen House really helped to get a feeling for what they put down in the history books, about Lincoln and the way things were then." —High School Senior

"D.C. has changed a lot in the last five years. The Kennedy Center probably made the greatest difference in cultural life." —Antique Dealer

"The Kennedy Center is a really marvelous idea . . . I mean, they have plays, concerts, opera, and even films . . . all in one big complex. You know, there are very few places in the United States—let alone the world—that offer just so much in one building that's so, so regal, so elegant really . . ." —High School art teacher

"And inside, it's like a million jewels all lighted and beautiful . . ." —Seven-year-old girl

"My favorite museum is the Air and Space Museum which was just opened not too long ago. Their museum has it all, from the men in the old days when they jumped off cliffs trying to fly, to the Wright Brothers at Kitty Hawk, Lindbergh's flight and spaceships. And they have the best movie "To Fly" which is so real; it's about flight balloons to fast planes to space modules, and they show it on this huge screen and believe me it is very exciting and very real." —Restaurant Owner

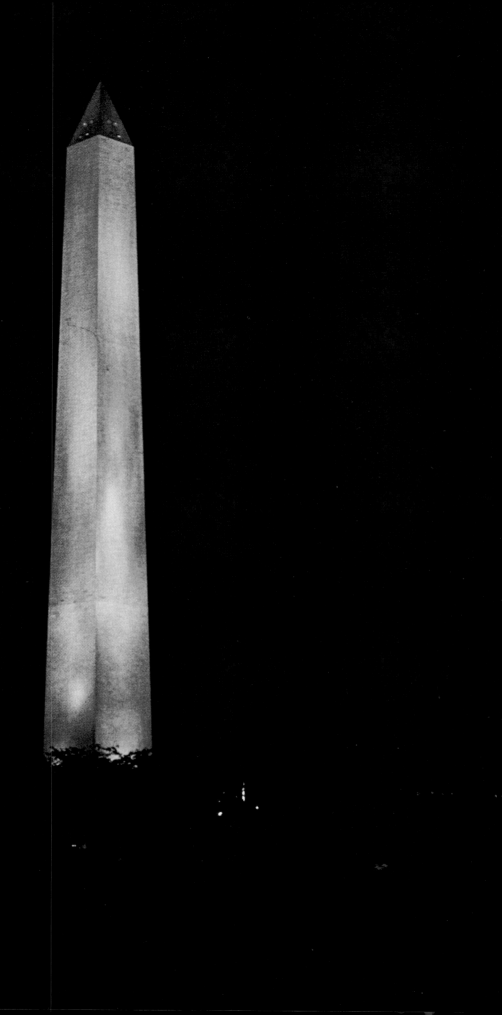

"I feel this is not only the capital of the U.S., but I feel this is the capital of the world. No other city can come close to what Washington has to offer its people. It's the land of opportunity right here in Washington. So many jobs are available— for all levels of working people. So many businesses one can get into . . . so many interesting people living here that you can see almost every day." —Real Estate Salesman

"Being from Chicago, everything we see about Washington is on the news, like with John Chancellor in front of the White House or the Capitol or something. Then we go walking around the White House going, "Wow, it's for real!" We've only been here for three days, but hey, we've had a good time." —Seventeen Year Old Tourist

"One of the things we wanted to do was to listen to a Congressional hearing and we found out that they publish all the topics in the Post every day that are going to come up . . . when we went to see a Senate hearing for the first time it was a real thrill and you just thought of all the people who have been in Washington over the years and all the decisions that have been made right here that affect the entire country." —New York Bus Driver

"This is a city where people are very conscious of issues and their rights. The human rights movement . . . gay rights, right-to-lifers . . . minorities . . . you name it and they have an organization here. People are very up front about getting action for their cause." —Grant Consultant, EPA

"The tour here at the capitol was the highlight of my trip . . . because it was the seat of our government, that's why I felt it was most important."

—High School Student, New Jersey

"With the different presidents . . . there's not a real change in the looks of the city, but the people change, they get concerned, like right now with Carter, they want to stay with their American roots." —Electrician

"There's a lot of excitement here, it's like the monuments send out light over the city in the evening . . . and all the ceremonies and parades and the President coming and going . . . it makes my head spin thinking about it." —Secretary

"They say around the country . . . the cities are dying . . . I say, 'Come to Washington.'" —Architect

"I guess it's only natural because of the government being right here and all, but most people are very aware of the news and who makes the news, sure people talk about the weather and sports, but they know what's happening in the world. At 11:00 everyone is glued to their TV, at a party all the action will stop at 11:00 and everyone will sit around and watch the news, people don't want to miss anything."

—Advertising Executive

"It's very beautiful . . . very clean . . . the way the city's laid out, it's very winding, but at the same time there's a lot of sort of circular paths that are like a continuous park. You never get the feeling that you're in a massive city of concrete. It's the historical with the modern." —Artist

"There are always new people coming into the city, every administration brings in new people of course, but I think a lot of people find Washington to be a very romantic city, exciting, sophisticated, very cosmo . . . people move here, especially young people in their 20's and 30's, for the good pay and the atmosphere."

—Engineer, Pentagon

"One of the highlights of the city is the Supreme Court, not only architecturally, but because it represents the judicial system which I associate with the roots of the country and our Government." —Librarian

"The thing I love most about working for the Treasury Department is knowing I am directly involved with the most essential part of the government: the economy."
—Accountant, Treasury Department

"As the oldest of the government department buildings, the Treasury is certainly imposing."
—Congressman

"I'm going to law school and I hope to live in Washington for the rest of my life. When I walk around Capitol Hill . . . the Supreme Court and the Senate Buildings, the Embassies, it seems deceptively serene; there is no apparent sign of activity or urgency. Here in Washington there is a constant reminder of certain ideals on which our country rests . . ."

—Law Student

"I'm from New York originally and I chose to live in Washington, well, just because it was the political center. And you know, after twenty-seven years here, I still believe in it. Working for the government is exciting, vital really. I mean working for a corporation on Wall Street just doesn't have that sense of history."

—Economic Consultant, HEW

"The National Archives is a must." —Lawyer

". . . Washington is so clean and beautiful . . ." —Schoolteacher

"The Hirshhorn Museum is absolutely unique . . ." —Art Student
"I just love sightseeing." —Retired Seaman

"Washington is the center of the world . . ." —Georgetown University Professor

"The Australian Mission really encourages Americans to visit." —Australian Embassy Receptionist

"In this city history becomes real . . ." —<small>White House Staffer</small>

"I think everyone appreciates the history of the city . . . the buildings that have survived way back to the time the British burned the Capitol . . . and the White House itself that has gone through so many changes . . . the National Archives which holds the records of the country's past, it's all there from the time of the slave ships to the Civil War and up to the present." —<small>Newspaper Columnist</small>

"I like the artistic beauty that is displayed in the old carpentry. The historic buildings are great because they all have a story behind them and you don't see that very often in other cities. Like I said, it's the beauty of the old carpentry . . . it's a lost craft . . . this is what they're trying to restore." —**Native Born Bookkeeper**

"Washington is the most beautiful city on the East Coast. It has building height limits so there are no towering skyscrapers. There is no heavy industry so there is little pollution. It's a natural area with a beautifully laid out architectural design by L'Enfant with one of the largest urban parks, Pierce Mill, which even has an operating grist mill. Quiet streets . . . wide green spaces . . . it's a magnificent city."

—**Research Scientist**

"There's a lot of neighborhood feeling . . . there's the Downtown crowd, the Capitol crowd, and the Georgetown crowd. You have to have a heavy date to go out of your neighborhood on a Saturday night." —Receptionist

"I would say Washington was the Hollywood of the East." —Lawyer

"Well, I would say the worst thing about Washington is that we don't have a baseball team, but when football season comes around, everybody is out there rooting for the Redskins . . . people here are very sports conscious in general, you always see people jogging in the parks or down by the C & O, and if they're not jogging they're riding bikes, or playing soccer or frisbee." —Accountant

"This city has a personality that sets it off from other cities in the country . . . in a way the whole country stands behind the city or should." —Statistician

"You can live the good life here." —Embassy Translator

"I was born here. I was born where the new Senate Office Building is on First Street. I lived there for 20 years. I was born right where the Vice-President's office is, and I went to all the neighborhood schools . . . I've seen a lot of changes in this city . . . a lot of good changes . . . this is a city of the people." —Gardener, Parks Department

"You know, there are real people living in Washington, too . . .
We aren't all Senators . . ." —Bus Driver

"This can be a real restful city . . ." —Retired Schoolteacher

"I grew up in the Midwest and I always thought that that was the best place because of the people, you know, but then I came to Washington thinking that I wouldn't stay more than a year or so, but boy! did I change my mind fast. There's excitement downtown and a lot going on, but if you live in Georgetown the way I do, you can go home to the beautiful old houses and relax with your friends; there's a lot of different sides to living in Washington." —Architect

"This is going on my second year in D.C. and I love it. The aesthetics I find very attractive, especially in Georgetown. Really the people within the environment make it what it is—very nice . . . very proud of their community and very anxious that it maintain its old charm and quality that has existed here for so many years."
—Law School Student

"Georgetown is the best place. It's like Europe. People are walking around, eating . . . you feel free, nobody pushes you. It's a leisurely way of life . . . that's why everybody comes here." —Secretary

"Going to school at Georgetown is a gas. We're set off up on the hilltop, but if you just walk down M street until you hit Pennsylvania Avenue and then you have everything . . . the downtown area used to be all office buildings but now there's a good blend, a lot of places to shop, restaurants, it's a little more liveable than it used to be . . . everyone's pretty fashion-conscious, there's a lot of glamour, but most people want to have fun, with all the things the city has to offer, it's not hard." —Georgetown University Student

"The people here in Washington have a lot to offer each other . . . we've got a lot of different kinds of people . . . the tourists who come and you hear them say how much they love the city . . . and the college kids from Georgetown and George Washington who really get into the city . . . and the Black people have a long history here ever since they came in from Maryland and Virginia to work on the construction of the Capitol. It's here for everyone to be proud of. It's something everyone has a part in because it's the real American heritage." —Insurance Salesman

"There's so many different sides to Washington . . ." —Secretary, Justice Department

"We've got so many statues and parks here . . . I've lived here for five years and I haven't seen them all yet." —Receptionist, Iranian Embassy

"*. . . Washington is a city of contrast . . .*" —Musician
"*. . . Inside and out, the Justice Department is very commanding . . .*" —Paralegal

or see h

"I'm a native Washingtonian and this is a beautiful city. All our parks with the flowers are gorgeous, and have you seen Constitution Avenue at night with the lights on? It's beautiful, just absolutely beautiful." —Housewife

"This is a beautiful city, a beautiful city. So many places to go, so many things to do all the time, so many things that are free." —Grocer

". . . the streets are clean." —Manager, Movie Theater

"Lincoln Park is a place for people, statues and pigeons . . ." —Social Worker

"We've got a lot of the classic styles of architecture here. Take the Executive Office Building for instance. Now, some people like the rococo style and some don't, but you have to agree that it's a fine example of its kind . . . the sort of thing you just don't see too much of anymore." —Insurance Salesman

"Washington reminds me a lot of Paris . . . you don't have all those skyscrapers blocking the view." —Capitol Policeman

"In the spring it's gorgeous here with the flowers and cherry blossoms, in the summer the parks are great when it's hot and you're feeling lazy, and in the fall and winter there's so much activity and excitement . . . that I never leave the city, even on vacations." —Assistance Director, Tourist Aid Agency

"The C & O Canal, now that has a lot of history to it; you can still go down and see the mules pull the Canal Clipper on the weekends . . . and if you feel like splurging you rent a boat out for a party . . . —Guard, Treasury Building

"Right now there are big plans to restore the waterfront, you know, more parks and green places and flowers instead of the old junk yards that used to be there."

—**Hairdresser**

"I like to work here. Why? Well, the money's good. Since they opened up those new tunnels it's easy to get here, so I meet lots of people." —Guard, FBI Building

"It's not hard to find a job here. There's always something to do, Georgetown's growing up now—all the new buildings and so forth. In a few years it's going to be something." —Bus Driver

"This is an ideal place to find a job, especially for young people. Everyone should leave home and try it on their own . . ." —Picture Framer

"I got my first job in Washington years ago, and have stayed on ever since. I find there is a truly unusual elegance to the city." —Art Historian

"I was up in Cape Cod last weekend and I started to talk about a lot of things that had come up in the news that week . . . and no one knew what I was talking about. It's incredible, in Washington everyone knows what's going on. I guess people are just more informed here than other places. —Guy Friday

"I can't complain . . . I've done well here." —Senate Mail Clerk

121

"*The metro is going to change everything . . . gettin' around town is going to be a piece of cake.*" —Jr. High School Baseball Coach

"Down on Seventh Street you can go to the Eastern Market. On Saturdays it's really fun, you see the open-air stalls and the farmers there with their vegetables and things . . . they're really friendly, they want to talk to you, find out how things are going. They'll talk about politics, Carter, how their business is going, what their children are doing in school . . . going down there gives you a good feeling.'' —Photographer

"Sure, Washington ain't no fairyland . . . but there's life here in the streets . . . we're special people . . .'' —Cab Driver

"This city has been home to me and my family for the past twenty years. I've seen a lot of presidents come and go; I've seen a lot of change and a lot of concern for the city by the people who live here . . . with all the restoration projects and the young people settling down and working hard, the city's got to come out ahead.''

—Court Stenographer, Supreme Court

"In the summertime they have the outdoor concerts and I like to go and sit . . . and just enjoy the music." —Retired Social Worker

"I moved here from Portland, Oregon, two years ago. I'm really not a city person and I was afraid it would be crowded and dirty and too urban, but then I came . . . and right away started noticing how green it was and the country so close by . . . I'm very happy . . ." —Researcher, Pentagon

"The Smithsonian has some fantastic pictures showing how things used to be along the Potomac . . ." —Museum Guard

"I never leave the city, even on the weekends. I'm always afraid I'll miss something, isn't that silly?" —Waitress

"That panda—that's our Chinese peace panda . . ." —High School Student

LIST OF COLOR PHOTOGRAPHS